Miraculous Psychotherapy

ACHIEVE YOUR ULTIMATE HAPPINESS WITH A COURSE IN MIRACLES

Gary Tiemann, LCSW

EDITING, DESIGN & PRODUCTION

Fearless Literary Services
www.fearlessbooks.com

CONTENTS

INTRODUCTION

Does It Ever Seem Like the World is Insane?

GOOD NEWS: The world *is* insane! This is good news because it means you're perceiving things correctly. That's not easy to accomplish, and it means you may feel so out of step with the world, and the people around you, that you'll be tempted to start doubting yourself. You can easily start thinking, "Maybe I'm the one who's crazy."

So let's take a look at just a few random bits of evidence of the world's insanity.

The fate of the world may rest on a popularity contest. Maintaining the most powerful military force the world has ever known, the United States elects a person to be in charge of such power through an election process that's basically a popularity contest. The outcome of that contest can turn on how well a candidate comes across in thirty-second soundbites. And those soundbites are broadcast by a media system that is more concerned about profits than revealing the truth. The popularity contest winner is placed in charge of an arsenal that can annihilate the world many times over. (And some of the most powerful weapons are called "peacekeepers.") Insane as that may sound, this "American way" is less crazy than some others!

Love, romance, and marriage don't work very well. Traditionally, our culture has placed a powerful emphasis on falling in love so that we can become ready to publicly promise our eternal love and devotion to one another — vows which fail over 50% of the time. We promise to love and honor forever, unless we decide at times to kill each other. Or we sing romantic songs about how "it must be love" because of how bad it hurts.

Sometimes religion just makes things worse. Disillusioned by love and patriotism, perhaps you decide to place your faith in religion. Isn't that where one finds a "saving grace"? Except that there are so many faiths from which to choose — and some of them will tell you, in no uncertain terms, that you're risking eternal damnation if you choose wrongly. Others will threaten to kill you right now for having chosen wrongly, because you're an infidel. Almost all of them will tell you, at least, that God loves you — but it's a love that seems to come with a lot of conditions.

So this is where we psychotherapists come in. We're supposed to be expert at defining and sorting out your anxieties about the world's insanity. We are part of the "healthcare industry" that deals with such things, and we are driven by science, practicing "evidence-based medicine." Perhaps you've engaged our services, and I hope it was helpful. It often is. I can truly say that the vast majority of the people I have known in my profession are kind, genuinely well-intended professionals who have only good will towards all they work with.

But there is no single, scientifically proven superior way in which to practice psychotherapy. The two chief icons of our profession, Sigmund Freud and Carl Jung, were truly well-intentioned pioneers and were doing the best they could, but they developed diverging points of view and methodology that persist in today's different approaches to the work.

The perspective of Freud, who was always concerned with the acceptance of psychoanalysis by mainstream medicine, is still the cornerstone of therapeutic practice today. Jung, his protégé, felt that in order to effectively address the anxiety that plagued humanity, one had to consider the mystical and spiritual aspects of our being. This was in large part because he had experienced so-called "supernatural" phenomena personally, and would not simply rule them out as unworthy of scientific exploration, as Freud did. Thus they eventually came to a parting of the ways, creating a divergence in therapeutic practice that is still with us today.

I am a Licensed Clinical Social Worker (LCSW) practicing psychotherapy, a career that seems like it chose me, rather than the other way around. Through my career I have watched the psychiatric community move increasingly toward physical and biological explanations, and pharmaceutical remedies. Ideas that address the spiritual or mystical approach to psychological healing are generally ignored.

Not only could I not ignore them, but increasingly found

these ideas fascinating and helpful. For instance, Buddhism raises the idea that "all suffering is in the mind, and when you learn to think clearly, all suffering ends." That sounds very much like the work of psychotherapy, but the Buddhists have been studying this idea in a formal and disciplined way for about 2600 years. Perhaps we should consider what they have to offer.

One of my most powerful influences is *A Course In Miracles* (ACIM), a modern psycho-spiritual teaching first published in the mid-1970s that has since been distributed in over twenty translations around the world, reaching millions of readers. Comprising a lengthy Text, Workbook of 365 daily meditations, and a brief Manual for Teachers, the Course was recorded by means of an "inner dictation" heard by Dr. Helen Schucman, a psychologist at Columbia University, with the assistance of her supervisor, Dr. William Thetford. After ACIM itself was complete, Schucman wrote down some peripheral pamphlets, including Psychotherapy: Purpose, Process and Practice. The first two sentences of that work state: "Psychotherapy is the only form of therapy there is. Since only the mind can be sick, only the mind can be healed."

I was hooked. As a therapy professional who's been studying spiritual approaches including ACIM for thirty years, I'm convinced that this perspective is essential to healing. I'm offering this book for all those who are interested in learning how to think more clearly — because it is in the enhancement of inner clarity that our ultimate happiness lies.

CHAPTER 1

Three Steps to Start Your Path to Happiness Immediately

WHEN clients come to my office, they are seeking. They may not be clear about their search, but ultimately they are looking for happiness. As their psychotherapist and a fellow human being, I want to help them find their happiness as best I can, beginning in the first session.

However, formal psychotherapy takes a lot of time, beginning with the necessary history taking, assessment, and planning of a course of treatment. So I developed a three-step assignment to help everyone get started on their path to happiness on their own. Regardless of your unique situation, you can apply these steps to your personal circumstances and your seeking. You may find them helpful right away, or you may notice that change comes gradually. But to jump-start your own spiritual process, here are three steps to follow while you are learning what is offered throughout the rest of this book.

STEP 1:

Practice gratefulness.

As often as you can, and in every way possible, practice gratefulness. As you learn, you will increasingly realize that everything has been given to you by the grace of God. We experience limits and deprivation only when we choose the ego mind over that inherent grace.

One of the main lessons of spiritual evolution is simply learning to recognize the part of our mind that the Course defines as "ego." When we live in our ego mind we are choosing limits; in fact we are choosing to have our lives defined by the experience of scarcity. The idea and the experiences of scarcity lead to fear; fear is the opposite of the consciousness of abundance. When you are experiencing abundance within, the natural response is gratefulness. Even if you are not really feeling this abundance, you can practice gratefulness anyway. In psychotherapy this is called the strategy of "fake it till you make it." Practicing gratefulness is the most direct way I know to align yourself with the consciousness of abundance. In turn, this helps reduce the tendency to believe in limits.

I also find it helpful to assume that reincarnation is real, meaning that you will eventually realize the truth of your infinite abundance. The only question is how many lifetimes it will take for you to realize that gift. The truth of your abundance quietly awaits your discovery and acceptance. I find it frustrating that my profession continues to ignore the compelling evidence of reincarnation, but more on that later.

For now, please trust that it is true. There can be no other outcome than eventually learning your inheritance of abundance over many lifetimes. Be grateful!

Step 2:
Focus only on doing the next right thing, based on a commitment to honesty and love.

This is certainly easier said than done! First of all, this step requires focusing on the present moment. The Buddhists have long understood the necessity of living in the present moment; many of their meditation practices develop the skills to do that. The ego part of our mind is constantly trying to seduce us into thinking of the past with regret, or planning for the future with anxiety. The ego mind wants us to do anything but live in the present moment, for there it literally does not exist.

The second part of this step, to proceed always with love and honesty, may not seem so hard. But if a child asks you if Santa Claus is real, will you choose love or honesty? Perhaps you have experienced such an encounter, and had to fashion an answer that was loving, when the black and white facts of the answer would be so disappointing to the child. A more consequential dilemma might be a physician confronted with sharing treatment options with a patient who is seriously ill. Just mentioning the possibility of severe side effects can increase the likelihood of the patient experiencing such effects. Again, the most truthful approach may not be the most loving one.

This points to the basic fact that this whole worldly dimension, by its fundamental nature, is an irreconcilable phenomenon. It is impossible to reconcile even the best intentions with the illusory nature of the world in a way that fulfills your ultimate happiness. In physics, the Heisenberg uncertainty principle demonstrates that defining one quality of a subatomic particle (speed) eliminates the ability to define another quality of that particle (location), and vice versa. You cannot know those two things at the same time. This "irreconcilable phenomenon" is just one example of the impossibility of making sense of the world as we normally perceive it.

Likewise, we encounter irreconcilability when we pursue such seemingly congruent values as love and honesty. The ego offers the seductive belief that we can make this world work, but we cannot. It urges us to focus on worldly goals that can only fail. Then we wonder what's gone wrong. This is why Buddhism instructs its followers to "let go of all worldly attachments." Our goal is ultimate happiness, which cannot be achieved with investment in worldly mechanisms and outcomes.

Our focus should always be on intentions rather than results, and our intentions should reflect our true mind. Our true mind knows that only the experience of love and truth is of any consequence. That's because this experience expresses our true mind, the part of us that was created in the image of God. The true mind knows not of separation, but only unity and wholeness with everything. This is the only state of mind that can work to bring us inner happiness. Paradoxically, this state of mind has a positive effect on the external, finite world because more of the Truth will be reflected in your worldly experience, especially in relationships.

Your present circumstance in time is a reflection of your state of mind. Unless you're very unusual you will experience dramatic contrasts and paradoxes in that state. One of my favorite tools to keep perspective in this regard is the image of the "laughing Buddha." He understands the illusory and irreconcilable nature of this dimension, but he also understands that his true nature is infinite perfection and happiness. The laughing Buddha is able to see and understand what appear to be limits — which are the source of all suffering — as the ego's delusions. From this perspective, all limits and their attendant suffering are utterly absurd, and the only natural response to that absurdity is amusement and laughter.

From the perspective of the laughing Buddha, time — a fundamental limit of our worldly experience — is absurd. If we can remember to laugh, we can usefully participate in the illusion of time and space while recognizing its false nature. It's this kind of paradoxical awareness that enables us to stay focused on "the now," and thus do the next right thing with love and honesty. (Notice the absurdity even in saying now and next like they are sequential experiences. I hope you are laughing!)

Honesty requires that we acknowledge where we are according to Truth, but also where we think we are according to the ego. Love requires that we respond to the ego by doing the next right thing, even as we acknowledge the passage of time as an illusion.

Another task of this step requires the recognition that your chief responsibility is your own state of mind. It is your job to love yourself, but not to the point of ignoring others' well-being. Where you draw the line between self-love and compassion can be very confusing, providing another example of the irreconcilability of this dimension. The key is letting go of our illusion of control, and trusting that Grace will take care of the circumstances for all concerned in the most productive and loving way.

Everyone is on the path of learning how to trust their connection to divine truth for everything they need. Eventually everyone will recognize this path. The ego wants you to believe you have to be in control in order to feel secure, but the path to enlightenment means learning to surrender any fear of your needs not being met. You will come to understand that you will always have what you need when you need it by the grace of God. By having no concerns about your own needs, your life becomes a celebration and your interaction with others is about sharing that celebration.

But while you are still on your path, you will experience anxiety, and you have to be honest about that. You also have to be kind to yourself. As the Course itself suggests, when a small child awakens from a nightmare with fear and anxiety, love requires responding to them with compassion and comfort. You wouldn't respond to the child by saying how ridiculous the nightmare was. Recognizing your own fear as an expression of the childish ego, love requires responding to that part of your mind with love and compassion.

STEP THREE:
Always forgive yourself and others for failures and shortcomings.

You will not be able to do the first two steps perfectly. Therefore, when you make a mistake, simply forgive yourself and resume your practice as best you can. Do not focus on shame or guilt about any mistakes, as a matter of fact — whether the mistakes belong to you or others.

The only purpose shame and guilt can serve is to let you know when you have strayed from love and honesty. The ego would have you wallow in guilt, which is an excellent way to avoid change. That's why the best response to recognizing error is to resume doing the next right thing with love and honesty. The ego, in its powerful and cunning ways, will try to seduce you to waste time and energy in self-destructive pursuits. So, forgive that as well.

Shame and guilt are destructive, chaotic energies; love and truth are unifying energies. Until we achieve our Atonement (the remembrance of being at one with all creation) the need to unify our energies exists. The path to enlightenment is simply returning all your thoughts and energies to the singularity of the infinite mind. Whenever you stray from that path, the only effective response is forgiveness. In the practice of love and forgiveness we find our way back to the singular truth of perfect love.

I know that these ideas are extraordinary, and if you find them confusing at this point don't despair. Grace is with you in ways you cannot begin to comprehend. As you practice these steps you will begin to notice that life becomes less burdensome. You will probably also notice subtle and not-so-subtle synchronicities, or meaningful coincidences. With time and practice, it will become easier for you to accept and trust that the inner power, which the Course calls the Holy Spirit, is in charge. It will also become easier to recognize that difficult experiences are taking you somewhere you want to go even if the destination is unclear.

The rest of this book elaborates on these three fundamental steps. Included in this elaboration are stories from my life that led me to the understanding I'm sharing with you now. Let me state clearly that what I have to share reflects the Truth that is not of my own making, but a gift of Grace for which I'm grateful.

CHAPTER 2

The Drama Triangle, and Other Games the Ego Plays

PERHAPS you are beginning to see that you possess a split mind. One part of your mind believes that you are separate from your source, consequently experiencing the world as a realm of separation. That perspective is the genesis of all limits and all fear, and the part of your mind that believes it is the ego.

The other part of your mind knows of no limits and consequently no fear. It experiences your connection to everything, and sees only reflections of love, truth and beauty. The Course calls that part of your mind the Holy Spirit. Free will means that you get to choose what aspect of mind you will rely upon.

You may not have even been aware of your split mind before your search for truth led you to sense it. Here, I want to outline for you the basic games the ego uses to seduce and keep you in bondage. As ACIM states, the ego would have you "seek but not find." Recognizing these ego games for what they are allows you find what you are truly seeking.

One of my favorite psychological tools is called Karpman's

Drama Triangle. A brilliant psychiatrist and practitioner of Transactional Analysis, Dr. Karpman created a simple diagram of a triangle with three points labeled Victim, Persecutor, and Rescuer. (I use a close adaptation in which I replace "Persecutor" with "Perpetrator.")

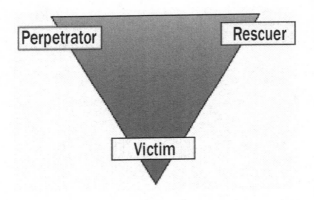

The Buddha's first Noble Truth was that "Life is suffering." Buddhism also teaches that we suffer because of our ego-driven attachments, but the ego does not want you to see that. Instead, in this game, it argues that your suffering is the result of victimization; that is, you suffer because someone or something has hurt you. Once that belief is accepted, your mind can easily become preoccupied with finding and identifying your "perpetrators." A Perpetrator can appear to be "real" as a specific person or calamity, or it can be a more general product of imagination. Ironically, the ego mind that creates the idea of limits is unlimited in its seductions. It will make up anything to obscure your perceptions so that you think of yourself as a victim.

Once you have identified yourself as a Victim and identified some kind of Perpetrator, you have essentially disempowered yourself. Now, your world is perceived and experienced as the sum total of what's being done to you. If the world is something that is done to you, and you are suffering as a result, then any possible relief would also have to be done to you. Thus, enter the Rescuer.

Depending on what melodrama of life you are caught in, the Rescuer is identified accordingly. For children, the Rescuer may be a parent. Facing illness, it may be a physician. Seeking romance, the Rescuer is a lover. And the greatest Rescuer of all may be a God who is separate from you.

In psychology we use the term "projection." ACIM teaches us that everything in this world is a projection, but in psychology that term is specific to the phenomenon of assigning traits, motives, and characteristics to people according to our definitions of who they are, instead of recognizing the truth of other individuals. Most of this happens at an unconscious level, and people don't realize they are doing it. It is a favorite tool of the ego to define and redefine people (including yourself) to serve its purposes from moment to moment.

Interestingly, those you define as Rescuers can become Perpetrators if they don't rescue you perfectly, according to the dictates of the perceived drama at the moment. These identifications are shifted around by the ego to accommodate its always-unstable delusions. This happens pretty frequently because the ego actually stacks the deck against its own Rescuers, by frequently shifting from blaming others to blaming yourself for suffering. Then you may become your own Perpetrator. Shame implies that you are flawed in a way that prevents your happiness, even if you find Rescuers. Thus, happiness is possible for others but not for you, because of your fatal flaw.

Guilt, on the other hand, implies you have the capacity for happiness but you are using your ability in a flawed way. You're just doing something wrong, so you should try harder. Guilt at least allows for hope in that you can change your behavior, whereas shame implies that is just the way you are with no hope of change. Projection is primarily an outwardly directed mechanism, while shame and guilt are internally directed. The ego can seduce you either way.

Learning to think clearly is the remedy for both. You may find yourself gyrating from the energy of grandiosity — that is, the idea that with enough enthusiasm and effort you can make this world work, or appear to work— to the depths of depression, wherein you're convinced that the world is hopeless and all your efforts to find happiness will be for naught.

I cannot emphasize enough how opportunistic the ego is. When blaming Perpetrators doesn't work to resolve suffering, it will resort to seeking Rescuers — then become bitterly disappointed with their inadequacies. Either way, you are imprisoned in the victim's mentality, and a long imprisonment can make one feel bitter, evenly violently so. Understanding this, it's easier to understand how some people can commit the atrocities they do, to themselves as well as others. They rationalize that striking out is the inevitable cost of the always-elusive goal of happiness. Such decisions are usually made on a subconscious level, though, because the ego does not want us to be fully conscious of what we do.

The Game of Sadomasochism

Many in my field have recognized the human tendency toward sadomasochism, which arises from the conviction that the illusion of power and control the ego experiences in punishment outweighs the suffering it causes. When we create suffering for others, it is sadism; when we create suffering in ourselves it is masochism. Greater suffering is interpreted by the ego as proof of more power, and thus becomes more satisfying.

The ego's seduction is ultimately about having power over the illusion of space and time, not just power over other people or our life circumstances. The ego attempts to convince us that we control everyday "reality" when in fact we do not —and cannot, because that supposed reality is actually the sum total of our unreliable perceptions. But the ego tells us that with that illusionary power and control, we can find our happiness. And the attempts to exert control may take many forms besides overt sadomasochism.

For instance, someone diagnosed with obsessive-compulsive disorder (OCD) may be obsessed about germs. Typically such people are very careful to avoid germs by avoiding handshakes or doorknobs. They may wash their hands so frequently, or use so much antibacterial lotion, that it is painful and harmful to their hands. OCD sufferers may recognize that their behavior is dysfunctional, yet they still get some sense of power and control that momentarily reduces their anxiety with each evasive behavior.

What they usually don't recognize is that their recurrent anxiety is a reflection of the general angst that comes from trying to control the entire experience of everyday life. The ego's blinders keep them from recognizing this deeper existential problem, riveting their attention on the ever-present threat of germs.

On the other hand, someone may be focused on going to work on time every day and doing a good job. They also may do well with their personal hygiene as well as cleaning their house. Perhaps they pay their bills and taxes on time. They keep their grass cut and hedges trimmed. And by typical standards they are labeled functional.

Getting Beyond "Normal"

Most of my profession is focused on getting people out of the dysfunctional category and into the functional category. But even the most "normal" and outwardly functional people may be dealing everyday with considerable angst and anxiety, and are unable to source their unease. So-called normal functioning promotes the ego's illusions that things are working. And yet, something's not quite right. The father of psychoanalysis, Sigmund Freud, seemed to recognize this when he asserted that the most therapy might be able to achieve was the transformation of a patient's "neurotic misery" into "common unhappiness."

For most, trying to attain more than normal unhappiness means intensifying the unproductive habits of the ego. They may choose to feel more victimized, or more guilty and ashamed, or seek to gain more power and control over people and circumstances. But none of these ego-driven strategies will ever lead to a sustained peace or happiness.

What does lead you out of all this unproductive turmoil? In a word, it is forgiveness. Remember, everything has already been given to you by the grace and love of God. But the confused thinking of the ego typically blocks our perception of this great gift. We want to experience power and control without realizing that we already have access to unlimited power; it just isn't of our own making, and it isn't about controlling the world, but our own minds.

Being created in the image of God, we have infinite power and therefore infinite control of our own awareness. The ego is not satisfied with knowing that power, it wants to pretend it is also the source of that power. To do so, it creates an entirely illusory world over which it paradoxically has no control. This leads to the insane predicament of pursuing infinite goals with finite means.

Forgiveness is the mechanism that dismisses and undoes these ego manipulations. Authentic forgiveness recognizes the unreality of all the games we play to maximize our misery and unhappiness in the pursuit of false power and control. In other words, authentic forgiveness is undoing. One of my favorite passages in ACIM states "you need do nothing." If you have everything, if you are everything, what is there to do? All that makes sense is to be grateful and celebrate all that you are and all that you have been given.

The vast majority of us think that we are confused, lost, and fighting to find happiness. The beginning of real psychotherapy is to recognize that condition, in order that we can begin to practice forgiveness. Forgiveness is the path to rediscovering the love that reflects your true nature. Even if others seem to persist in judging and blaming, you don't have to take it personally. A simple way to see through all the games of the human ego is to understand that anyone who is unkind is confused. "Forgive them for they know not what they do."

Sometimes I simply remind my clients that while the world as we typically see it is totally insane, we don't have to take it personally.

CHAPTER 3

What is the Level of Your Needs?

ABRAHAM MASLOW'S most famous contribution to psychology is his "hierarchy of needs." As a young researcher working with monkeys, he observed that some of the monkeys' needs took precedence over others. Eventually he expanded upon this basic research to construct a hierarchy applicable to the range of needs of human beings.

For instance, someone who is having trouble breathing is not going to be concerned about his or her hunger or thirst until the breathing problem is resolved.

Here is an outline of the "Hierarchy of Needs," in ascending order from the most basic, as it was first published in Personality and Motivation in 1954.

- First: biological and physiological needs. This includes air, food and drink, shelter, warmth, sex, and sleep.
- Second: safety needs. This includes protection, security, law, limits, stability.
- Third: belonging and love needs. This includes family, affection, relationships, working in groups.
- Fourth: esteem needs. These include achievement, status, responsibility, reputation.

- Fifth: self-actualization. This is the highest level and includes personal growth and fulfillment.

I think it is best to view this hierarchy as a general guideline that has exceptions, depending on individuals and circumstances. But it is a very useful tool for analyzing games the ego plays.

How Needs Lead to Fear

First of all, the ego seduces us with the concept of needs itself — the antithesis of the spiritual truth that we have been given everything. Need implies lack, and serves as a camouflage for fear. In fact, neediness is the genesis of all fear, and thus we can look at the hierarchy of needs as a stepladder to the transcendence of fear.

Remember, in this dimension we have a split mind. On one hand there is the mind created in the image of God, characterized by eternal, infinite love and perfection. On the other hand we have the ego, with its experience of duality within the bounds of time: life and death, beginnings and endings. The physical universe, being a projection of the collective albeit split mind, reflects both aspects of our mind. Our individual experience is a projection of our individual mind as it complements the collective mind, until we experience the transcendence that gives us the understanding that we are all of one mind.

Everything in the universe reflects both finite and infinite aspects. Existence appears to be limitless and without a beginning or end in time, yet somehow we are trapped in our stories of life and death within infinity. Enlightenment is essentially the process of learning to recognize your split mind, then choosing to align only with those symbols that reflect the infinite Truth. The symbols that reflect the ego are to be simply forgiven.

So in the beginning of our seemingly time-bound, individual life, we experience the ego's seduction of need with our first breath. We feel separate and alone as soon as we are expelled from our source, our mother. Thus begins the journey of fear and separation that will ultimately end in our recognition of being one with everything, with fear becoming unimaginable. Maslow's hierarchy of needs is an outline of this process. I believe he was recognizing a process of human development that A Course in Miracles can help us understand and follow even more effectively.

Grandeur vs. Grandiosity

Every step of the hierarchy presents you with fear reminding you that "something is not right." The ego tells you that's because there is some worldly thing, relationship, or circumstance that you do not have. Subsequently, we scramble to secure or achieve what we think we desire. When we do satisfy the longing for what we think we desire, we assume it was of our own doing.

As the Course points out, this is grandiosity. The only reason we appear to achieve anything is because all has been given, and we occasionally decide, consciously or unconsciously,

to accept or recognize some small portion of it. The experience and realization that we have been given everything
is grandeur, for which we can be truly grateful. But our
"achievements" are piecemeal symbols of the Gift of everything, as limited by the ego. And, as Maslow recognized,
when we achieve what we pursue there is partial satisfaction
— but it does not last. The angst of feeling something is still
not right returns, and the ego has an easy time seducing us
with a desire to pursue the next worldly thing we think we
don't have.

We go through this process, level by level, until there
is no worldly thing left the ego can offer. We evolve from
satisfying our individual needs to appreciating and serving
others' needs as well; we also evolve from concrete, material
needs to those that are more abstract. We become less at-
tached to the material world, and more rooted in the world
of the mind.

Even so, at every level the ego will continue to seduce
you with its games of victimization, shame and guilt. These
will only keep you preoccupied at lower levels, delaying your
evolution. So, becoming more aware of these ego games is
the most effective route to realizing the ultimate gift of joy
and happiness that you already possess, deep within.

We will experience the progress of Maslow's hierarchy
because it is inevitable that Truth will eventually supersede
ego. The infinite relentlessness of the gift of the Holy Spirit
will always outlast the limits of the ego that, paradoxically,
works hard to prevent its own success. The ego is insane!

Over the seemingly great span of time, karma engineers our hierarchical lesson plan, using as many lifetimes as necessary. Lessons mastered in previous lives are accumulated in the superconscious mind, allowing an easier transition through previously mastered levels.

Needs in Relationship

I would also like to elaborate on some of the specific vulnerabilities the ego induces in the context of relationships. As we ascend through the hierarchy of basic needs and approach the desire to experience intimate connections with others, the ego can take advantage in two ways. First, if we are experiencing longing, and we are not in a relationship, the ego easily seduces us with the conclusion that a relationship is needed. Then it can preoccupy us with all the drama and games of pursuit. If we are in a relationship and we become aware of longing or dissatisfaction, the ego has an easy time convincing us there is something wrong with the relationship, providing another entire scenario of drama and games.

There are enlightened people who choose not to participate in the vulnerabilities and distractions that are so prolific in the area of intimacy and relationships. Transcending the lessons in this realm of the hierarchy does not require a "successful" relationship; transcendence only requires thinking clearly about relationships. What's important to understand is that transcendence of intimacy needs has little to do with whether you choose celibacy or not, but with achieving clear thinking in your choice.

There is a Buddhist saying suggesting that "the remedy to loneliness is solitude." In other words, the ultimate solution to loneliness will not come from some worldly relationship, but from being at home within oneself. However, there is nothing wrong with having a partner who can share this home with you.

So let me emphasize that everyone will eventually achieve self-actualization, transcending all worldly needs and their attendant fears. Self-actualization is the awareness that you are connected to all there is, such that fear is no longer a factor in how you direct and live your life. I'm not aware if Maslow ever considered the role of reincarnation, but I think the idea helps us understand the time scale of truly transcending all our needs. The more you understand about this process, the easier it becomes to do the next right thing, to forgive those who are confused, and enjoy the rewards of gratitude.

CHAPTER 4

Learning to Grow
from Grief to Happiness

Elizabeth Kubler-Ross outlined "five stages of grief" that have become a cornerstone of psychology, familiar to all therapists. Here I will explain the role of the ego in the dynamics of this process. In this finite dimension, characterized by the duality of beginnings and endings, we are confronted with grief at almost every kind of ending. With the correct perspective, the suffering of grief can be reduced as you grow toward your ultimate happiness.

Stage I, denial, is the basic psychological mechanism of simply rejecting a hard truth that life presents us with. After all these years I am still impressed when I witness our capacity to look at something right in front of us and simply refuse to see it. The ego parades one worldly thing after another before us in its attempt to seduce us into believing we can make this dimension work. Everything the ego offers will ultimately fail and we will eventually recognize that failure — but only after we transcend our denial of the obvious.

When a truth that we don't like is first recognized, we will have a childish or regressive response of anger. This is stage II. We all have a primal attitude of "I want what I want when I want it, and if I can't have it, I'll get mad." This is the ego in its most raw and obvious form.

As we realize that anger itself is not productive, we begin trying to "fix" our situation so that we can have what we want. This is the third stage of grief, called bargaining. And with some kinds of loss or disappointment, our bargaining efforts may actually improve the situation.

However, an irreversible loss, such as the death of a loved one, confronts us with helplessness when we realize that there is no bargaining that can succeed. An overwhelming sense of hopelessness defines the experience of depression, the fourth stage of the grieving process. When most people think of grieving, this is the stage they are generally most aware of. In this stage, sadness and futility are finally processed.

The fifth and final stage of acceptance commences when the experience of depression has been "given its due," and one's experience of loss can be honored with an increasing sense of compassion. Following upon that, new opportunities for joy can be allowed and experienced. It is not that the loss has been forgotten, but simply that it does not interfere with the potential for new and life-affirming experiences. Now memories of the loss itself are not singularly experienced as sad. Memories involving the object of the loss, be it a person, pet, or any beloved thing, can be experienced as happy once again.

Applying the map to real life

This is a very straightforward and simplistic explanation of the grieving experience that we can map out theoretically. But in real life, it is never simple and straightforward. Life is a parade of beginnings and endings, constantly overlapping and convoluting in infinite and unpredictable ways. It is helpful to have a clear outline of the process of grieving, especially since it has so much to do with the evolution from ego to enlightenment.

The ego is the childish part of our mind that "wants what I want when I want it." Paradoxically, it can seduce us with seemingly more mature techniques, such as delayed gratification. But all its techniques ultimately serve that childish part of our mind. The ego attempts to seduce us with the idea that we are in control, or at least should be in control of our life circumstances in order to fulfill our wants and needs. Anything of a worldly nature that you may experience as a loss directly confronts the ego's love of control.

The ego, in its powerful and seductive ways, will try to prevent us from realizing that we are not in control of our worldly experience. It especially does not want us to realize that we would be better served by learning the skills of surrendering to Grace. Psychology has defined many of the ways by which we hold onto illusions of control; the simplest and most straightforward of these is denial. In fact, all defense mechanisms are essentially different flavors of denial. All of them serve the ego's delusion that you can be in control of something that, by its very nature, cannot be controlled.

Anger is a camouflage of fear. If you were to fully examine fear you would understand that fear is about not being in control of your happiness. When you are perfectly happy, you cannot be angry or afraid. When you are not happy, the ego wants you to believe there is something wrong with other people, or the world in general, without appreciating that the ego's own approach to life is what's going wrong. In fact, it is insane. So it has to blame something other than itself.

We get mad or angry with whatever the ego can seduce us into blaming. When we blame others we are entering the drama triangle through projections, and when we blame ourselves we are entering the dungeon of shame and guilt. If you recognized that you are not in control, you would begin to look at the alternative of surrender, which is the key to happiness. However, surrender is also the undoing of the ego. In this sense, forgiveness is not about fixing the ego's mistakes or problems; it is about dismissing the ego in a way that acknowledges its ultimate meaninglessness.

The final solution
Once we have tired of the blaming game, having indulged in all the self-deceiving gyrations the ego can invent, the only way out is the final solution of forgiveness. This means forgiving yourself and all others. On the surface, forgiveness may seem to be about letting someone off the hook for a particular transgression, when the real process is dismissing the ego's seductions. Ultimately it is an acknowledgment that our infinite Being cannot be threatened by any-

thing finite, or by the fear associated with anything limited or temporary.

In stage III bargaining, the ego reasserts itself by looking for worldly solutions to a perceived loss. If you achieve some satisfaction through these manipulated solutions and things seem to get better, the ego quickly claims it is a validation of its principles. But every bargain the ego proposes ultimately fails.

Truth is Truth. It quietly sits there knowing nothing can threaten it. Nothing can obscure it forever. Whatever camouflage is attempted will be temporary and when the dust settles, Truth will be there as clear and constant as it always has been.

This is why the death of a loved one is such an awkward and destabilizing force for most people. It is no surprise that our culture has such difficulty facing the fact of death. We do bizarre things, including the camouflage of dead bodies so they "look natural" and can "rest in peace." Western medicine has essentially declared war on death, sometimes perpetrating sadomasochistic treatments and behaviors that actually promote suffering in order to forestall the inevitable.

In stage IV, sadness or depression, the ego is temporarily defeated. The helplessness and hopelessness that provide the foundation of the ego is recognized, and the illusions of control are seen for what they really are. The intensity of depression experienced is in direct correlation to how deeply we've been seduced by the ego's illusions of control; if there were no illusions of control, there would be no sadness.

Working through every seduction

One by one, we can work through every seduction the ego throws at us, grieving each one until we surrender all illusions of control. Without the ego there can be no unhappiness; those who have surrendered their ego, like the laughing Buddha, have also surrendered all unhappiness. At this level there is only love for all others. There are no ego games of power and need, fear, shame or guilt. The individual at this level knows that by doing the next right thing with love and honesty, everything needed will be given by Grace when it is needed. And for those who still suffer, we feel compassion; this is why "Jesus wept."

Stage V is acceptance. Here the ego assesses its predicament and once again reasserts some games and seductions. However, it usually has to contend with at least some revelation of the truth during the grieving process. Perhaps the constancy of Grace was experienced to some degree, and in spite of the ego's best efforts, authentic happiness begins to emerge. Remember, happiness is your truth. The ego cannot hide it forever, and the gift of grieving is that it can take us another step further along the way to ultimate happiness.

So we meander through life, suffering reminders all along the way that we are not in control. Grace constantly offers you everything, and the ego constantly tries to interfere with that offering, preventing you from realizing the gifts of complete joy and happiness. Every grieving episode you go through takes you forward, however, and every step up the hierarchy of needs is a new level where the ego has to remodel its efforts. But you will ultimately transcend illusions, learning that nothing real, nothing truly of God, can be threatened, and all the joy and gifts bestowed by God are yours forever.

Seen in this light, you will recognize grief's gift is the mechanism the Holy Spirit uses to gradually awaken us from our nightmare of suffering. And for this you can be thankful.

CHAPTER 5

Are You Ready for a Teacher to Appear?

I N THIS dimension of space and time, we suffer the illusion of separation. Instead of understanding that we are one with everything and nothing can be "outside" ourselves, we experience an incompleteness that motivates us to seek love, peace, and understanding. We may also believe there is some kind of salvational knowledge that is as yet unknown to us, and can only be gained through the proper religious rituals, or our humble surrender to God or a "higher power." Even atheist scientists believe that there is no end to the knowledge yet to be gained through their own rituals of making hypotheses, devising experiments, and establishing double-blind confirmations.

"When the student is ready the teacher will appear," goes the old saying. Remember, Grace is constantly offering us everything. When we do not recognize that we have the gift of all, it is because of the interference our ego creates with its illusionary purposes and pursuits. But the finite nature of the ego is ultimately no match for the infinite persistence of Grace. Whatever the ego's vulnerabilities are, Grace will provide an appropriate teacher or series of lessons that perfectly fulfill what you need to learn at any given moment. We only need to learn to be open to instruction, and be willing to give up the ego's dictum: 'Seek and do not find." (ACIM, Text, Chapter 12, Section V).

The more you develop your conscious awareness of Grace, and the more you accommodate its gifts, the more peace and happiness you will experience. Sounds so easy! But the ego is persistent, and its sadomasochistic nature obscures the lessons we need to learn. Yet if you are willing, you can be guided on your path in ways that are far beyond your conscious understanding. Let me share some of my journey for illustration.

I've always been fascinated by the phenomenon of hypnosis. There are many powers of the mind that Western science and medicine have a hard time explaining, including many confirmed examples of major surgery being performed with no anesthesia and little discomfort or pain. Most people are familiar with the extraordinary demonstrations that stage hypnotists perform, without really contemplating the implications of the phenomena demonstrated.

At the beginning of my professional career in psychotherapy I thought I was just following a professional curiosity about hypnosis. Looking back now, I can easily see that I was being led by my own "internal teacher.' I was encouraged by an older, experienced colleague to pursue training with the American Society of Clinical Hypnosis (ASCH), considered by many to be the most respected institution on hypnosis.

In my introductory training I was introduced to such dissociative phenomena as Dissociative Identity Disorder (DID), popularly known as "multiple personalities." In retrospect, it doesn't seem like a mere coincidence that DID clients were showing up in my practice. I personally witnessed such strange phenomenon as xenoglossy, (speaking in a foreign language that is not consciously known), and physiological discrepancies, such as an older middle-aged client with arthritic knees happily sitting with her legs folded under her when a teenaged "alter" inhabited her body.

We understand from ACIM that while there may be many egos, there is only one true mind. We experience ourselves as separate and limited but the truth is that we are neither. Someone exhibiting DID replays this truth in their own microcosm; their ego-mind is split into multiple selves that are often unaware of the others. I've seen clients with fifty or more alters, and the literature documents cases of hundreds of alters within a single person's consciousness.

As with most mental health diagnoses, DID is not a black-and-white definition, but the recognition of a cluster of symptoms. The diagnosis can be validated only after a relationship is established with the client, enabling opportunities to expose alters in the safety of the office. Over the years I have worked with eight to ten cases of DID; on average, outpatient treatment requires ten to twenty years. I have worked with four or five DID clients intensely for that length of time.

Some DID patients have an alter that is clinically referred to as an "inner self helper" (ISH). The ISH is often described by the other alters thusly: "that one is never afraid," "that one is different from us," or, "that one knows everything." Once a legitimate ISH is defined, the therapist can utilize the ISH for treatment strategies, information and insight. I had a few that I worked with over the years, including two ISH's who provided extensive assistance.

One of them is called "Oracle" by her other alters; the other is referred to as "One" (ISHs usually have these kinds of names). Both Oracle and One would refer to me as the "teacher" for their respective host personalities and alters. On the other hand, Oracle and One taught me a great deal not only about their respective hosts, but also about the nature of life itself.

Their teachings included information about reincarnation. The issue arose with one client when, after years of work, she had achieved a relatively comfortable life situation after healing some severe early trauma. Yet at this point of relative comfort, she began experiencing a recurrence of nightmares about dying in a roller coaster accident. She had experienced this dream on and off throughout her life, beginning in early childhood. With the help of her ISH, it was determined that this was the cause of death in her most recent previous life.

We also learned that she died with her six-year-old son in that roller coaster accident. She was 29 years old at the time, in 1939 in the Northeast area of the United States. More significantly, it became clear that she felt so much shame and guilt about her son's accidental death that her superconscious mind placed her in a current lifetime situation involving forgiveness challenges including echoes of that previous incarnation. Needing to develop forgiveness for her mother was a projection mechanism for the forgiveness she needed for herself. Forgiveness thus not only heals current wounds and eases difficult relationship predicaments; it can also release karmic binds, allowing one to move forward in an evolutionary process toward ultimate happiness.

Whatever victim-perpetrator drama our ego conjures, in the course of one lifetime or over a span of lifetimes, the release of suffering is still provided by a forgiveness practice. Grace will lead us to those lessons and teachers as we need them, if we allow it to do so.

I recall one conversation with the ISH named One wherein she chided me: "You don't think it was an accident that she [the client] showed up in your office, do you?" With that ISH it was possible to have a very casual and even playful interaction after the seriousness of our purpose had been accomplished. The other ISH that I learned so much from had a more serious style, including a didactic yet nurturing voice.

Even in our dualistic ego-dimension, the line between student and teacher is not as distinct as we think it is. We can learn to appreciate that whomever comes before us serves as some kind of teacher. In this illusion of separation we think there is much outside of us to seek; Grace responds to our confusion in the most loving way, by meeting us where we are. If we think our answers are outside, Grace will respond with exterior teachers and situations that nonetheless lead us back to the truth of ourselves.

DID clients must come to terms with many "egos" within their one host personality system. Treatment strategy involves teaching them to be honest, kind and respectful to each other, just as they perceive each other separately. Therapist and client respect that each alter has a meaningful and even loving purpose that benefits the whole of their dissociated system. Once the system of alters recognizes the loving purposefulness of each alter and the contribution that each makes to the survival of the whole, some very difficult and apparently dysfunctional behaviors can be forgiven and internal cooperation becomes easier. With this cooperation the many alters in the system can learn to become whole and at peace.

Whether we learn from personalities that appear to be inside or outside ourselves, we are all being led with lessons and teachers that fit perfectly in our evolutionary process. Sometimes the labels student and teacher will be used to distinguish our particular functions and services, but even so the teacher is also a student, and the student is a teacher. We can learn to trust that Grace will lead the way, presenting perfect learning opportunities every step of the way. Accepting that everything and everyone who shows up is a gift in that respect, gratitude is the only natural and reasonable response.

CHAPTER 6

How I Learned about Miracles

So far, I have shared some of my enthusiasm about *A Course in Miracles* (ACIM). Let me share with you more of my own journey in this process.

I was first introduced to ACIM around 1990. At that time we had a small local bookstore that specialized in books about spiritual and psychological topics, where I often stalked the aisles. When I ran across the book there I was immediately drawn to it, but on beginning to read it I found it very confusing, and set it aside.

In 2004, I happened to hear a recorded lecture on Dr. Schucman's Pamphlet on Psychotherapy. Soon after that, a friend shared with me recorded information by Gary Renard. I listened to this before I became aware of his book *The Disappearance of the Universe* (referred to hereafter as DU). I happened to be driving on a four-hour trip, requiring a very early start with a particularly glorious sunrise. With a great deal of confusion, I found myself weeping as the recording started. I felt the release of something that I could not explain. So after having that experience, I was eager to read DU.

At the outset of this remarkable teaching memoir, Gary Renard explains that he was a middle-aged man and not very happy with his life circumstances. He decided to focus his energies on spiritual work, particularly meditation. One day, he came out of a meditation in his living room to find two strangers sitting on his couch. They had somehow manifested there, not walked in through the door like normal human beings. They soon identified themselves as "ascended masters" who had arrived to teach him about A Course in Miracles. They also told him that he would write DU, in order to help a greater number of people understand and benefit from ACIM.

The book first connected with me because of a couple amusing synchronicities. The first was seeing my own name frequently repeated as a participant in the mystical conversations that make up the book. Also, at the time Gary was married to Karen, now his ex-wife, who was described as not very spiritual in the book. My wife Karen has used those very words to describe herself.

Finally, Gary is told by his unusual teachers that in one of his previous lifetimes he was a disciple of a Native American leader in the Midwest, who was so revered by his people that they built a huge earthen mound for him to live on. Today that area is known as the Cahokia mounds. I spent the earliest part of my life in East St. Louis, Illinois, and then in the eighth grade my family moved to Collinsville, Illinois. Both communities border the Cahokia mounds. In my early years it was a park where we would sometimes play or, as teenagers, hang out; today, it is a revered archaeological site with limited accessibility to the public.

For these and many other reasons, I was hooked on DU, carrying and reading it wherever I went. I am a slow reader and don't usually enjoy the process of reading itself, preferring audiobooks when available. But I was devoted to Gary's story. It wasn't long after I finished DU the first time that I made my plans to tackle ACIM again. In my research I found that the Foundation for Inner Peace offered an unabridged audio version of ACIM on CDs. This was a very lengthy undertaking that would occupy a lot of my time, so I developed a routine of regularly listening to a CD while sitting in my hot tub under the stars at night. Considering how dry and itchy my skin became during that period, it probably wasn't the best plan! But the experience of listening to the Course under the stars while in the hot tub was too rich of an experience to cut short.

It took about a month to work my way through the audio recordings of the Course Text. Then I started the Workbook, and was very consistent about reading a lesson each morning. I'd also write the lesson on a sticky note and attach it to the dashboard of my truck, so I would remember it and think about it throughout the day.

After a month of this routine, I had "the dream": I was in a magnificent castle watching my wife sleep restfully on the floor. Not in physical form, I was observing everything from a very high place. And I was experiencing bliss beyond anything I had ever known or could have imagined. It was very clear to me that this was an affirmation of the spiritual work that I was pursuing. And it changed everything for me. One of my favorite passages from the Course is "brother, you do not know joy." I now understand that what we appreciate as worldly joy — even the best the world can offer — is nothing compared to the inner joy available to us.

I was also aware that the love I felt for Karen in the dream went far beyond any words I could use to describe it. In this dream my wife represented the whole of humanity, usually experienced as an incomprehensible number of separate individuals. As my partner in life she is my "other," representing anything that I perceive as not of me. And she was asleep, meaning that she symbolizes the whole of humanity that remains unaware of its spiritual reality. Being clothed in a nightgown meant that certain things would not be revealed; resting on the floor of the castle suggested that our sleep persists as long as we are rooted to earthly, worldly things. The intense love that I felt for her represented the intensity of the love I feel for all "others," even though I am not conscious of that in my normal, daily routine, at least not yet!

Of course, a dream is a picture of what's going on in our minds when the unconscious is freer from our waking ego's control. This dream was telling me about me. The most important aspect of the dream, transcending all the symbols and interpretations, is the experience of it.

All told, these early experiences with the Course, Gary's book, and my own inner process changed my life profoundly. I was becoming clearer about the ego's absurd offerings of contaminated joy and severely limited happiness — laughable gifts in contrast to what I now understand to be accessible in Spirit. I also came to understand that fear is merely a symptom of my confusion about who I really am, warranting further mind training and conditioning. Finally, I've grasped that I am not the creator of my happiness; it has been given to me. I can choose to accept it, or I can choose the path of the ego. Anytime I choose the ego, the singular remedy that completely corrects this mistaken choice is forgiveness. And ultimately all confusion will be forgiven. Now I know that whenever I choose to follow the ideas the Course has taught me, I am at peace. Unfortunately, my ego is persistent and in my confusion I forget those ideas. I understand the Buddhist teaching that "all suffering is in the mind, and when you learn how to think clearly all suffering ends." I know that A Course in Miracles is not the only path or practice that can teach one how to think clearly. But, I know that it does work and it's the most efficient path I'm aware of.

CHAPTER 7

Getting a Little Help
From My New Friends

IN MY perspective of Freud and Jung's personalities, Freud was very concerned about his work being accepted by the mainstream science community. Perhaps being Jewish in that area and era sensitized him to consequences of being an outsider. Or, maybe, it was simply the practical consideration that he needed his work and practice to support his lifestyle.

Jung, on the other hand, was not so encumbered. His personality was such that he easily listened to the beat of his own drummer regardless of what others might think. It didn't hurt that his wife's wealth provided them with a comfortable lifestyle.

The contrast between them is still reflected to this day in the mental health community.

There is an often quoted phrase in my profession: "evidence-based practice." Yet there is very little acknowledgment of the evidence of reincarnation and other such hard to quantify phenomenon as placebo and nocebo, paranormal phenomenon and the like. More and more I was abandoning some of the standard traditions that reflect more of Freud's ideas in my own practice and giving myself the audacity of Jung to follow my own path. I started speaking more frequently about these things and even introducing some of these things to clients.

So being in this quandary I started fantasizing about how nice it would be to have mentors like Arten and Pursah, the ascended Masters that show up on Gary Renard's couch, of my own. I would go to Gary's website to keep up with his schedule and opportunities that I might have to see him. It's amusing to remember that I saw an offer that he was available for individual phone sessions several times before I thought to call him. It may not be as dramatic as having future beings materialize on my couch, but Gary was a coach to whom I felt a deep connection — and a coach who does have future beings materialize on his couch! My prayer had been answered even if I was a little dense in recognizing it for a while.

So I started having occasional sessions on the phone with Gary. Most of the time these were just general discussions about ACIM and writing. There was nothing terribly profound in those phone sessions, but I was developing more of a relationship with Gary and a better understanding of ACIM. This also led to me hosting him to come do a workshop in Shreveport.

Gary and Cindy generally like to come in on Thursday for a Saturday workshop to accommodate any snafus that can happen when traveling. But when things work out as planned, that leaves Friday open. They generally like to keep it rather low-key that day so they can save their energy for the workshop. I planned on showing the two of them around town and taking them to eat at some of my favorite places.

On Friday morning, Gary was not feeling well. He elected to rest in the room for the day but Cindy was all for exploring Shreveport with me. I had only limited contact with her until this time so this was a real opportunity for us to get to know each other. I had heard that she was one of the kindest and warmest people you could ever meet and now I can validate that.

So in the process of showing her the sights and having lunch at one of my favorite places, we spent hours together sharing personal histories. She is very easy to talk to and I felt that same connection to her as I did with Gary.

Gary had disclosed in his books that the beings who materialize and coach him in his work and life are actually he and Cindy's future selves in their next lifetime. Gary is Pursah and Cindy is Arten. It was also disclosed in his books that they were disciples of J (most know him as Jesus). Gary was the disciple Thomas and wrote The Gospel of Thomas. Cindy was a lesser-known disciple name Thaddeus.

Cindy is also a trained psychotherapist and has a Masters degree in spiritual psychology. Her practice fits in with all that she does helping and traveling with Gary. She is also very intuitive and has some psychic ability. In our time together she acknowledged there was something about me that reminded her of the disciple John. She also told me of her friend Kevin Ryerson, the psychic and channeler who works with actress Shirley MacLaine.

The next day Gary and Cindy did a wonderful job with the workshop and everything went well. The following day I picked them up and took them to the airport for their departure. In saying our goodbyes I was as distraught as if I were saying goodbye to one of my kids with the expectation of not seeing them again for a long time. Once again, my emotional experience was undeniable but I really didn't understand.

After that visit and workshop it didn't take me long to start reading Kevin Ryerson's book *Spirit Communication*. While reading the book I applied, through his website, for a session. I was very anxious but excited. I have never done a psychic reading before, and a part of me was incredulous that I was doing all of this "strange" stuff. (I don't think Jung would have been so reluctant!) This does not fall under the "evidence-based practice" model. But I am now absolutely convinced of the phenomena of the paranormal and metaphysical, while being aware that there are unscrupulous people in these fields. I think it is necessary to have disciplined professionals involved in this research and work. I find Kevin Ryerson to be legitimate.

Kevin's instructions for phone sessions recommended using a land-line as they are considered more reliable. I thought my office phone, which had been switched to wireless, would be fine. The process is that when you call in Kevin answers and explains his process for a few minutes. Then he takes a moment and goes into a trance. At that point, I heard a very soft-spoken voice say a prayer, the voice of the

Gospel John. Kevin is the reincarnation of John. In a few moments a very strong and resonant voice announced that Ahtun Re had arrived.

He asked me what questions I had, and I started to explain the attraction and synchronicities I'd noticed with Gary and Cindy. He began to explain that in one of my previous lives I was a scholar, scribe or researcher who worked at the great library in Alexandria, Egypt and that Jeshua (Jesus) and his disciples, including Gary and Cindy in their previous lives, spent a great deal of time at that library. When he pointed out I personally knew Jeshua in that incarnation, the phone went dead.

When he said that, I felt an intense rush of energy in my body. It took me a moment to gather myself and figure out that I needed to redial the number and hope that we would reconnect. Ahtun Re answered and when I asked, "what happened?" he explained that my energy surge interfered with the electronics of the cell phone. Jung would have called it a "catalytic exteriorization phenomenon." That's what Kevin meant by suggesting that land lines are more reliable!

The rest of the session brought forth some interesting things about my past and my family. My wife is a CPA, and Ahtun Re said she worked at the Alexandrian library, managing the inventory. Very accountant-like! He also reported that I was an Essene and part of the Thomasine soul group. I wrote a book or gospel that in today's times is called the "lost Gospel Q." In researching and reading about that, I learned that there is no known copy of that gospel but it is agreed by many biblical scholars that it exists, based on the evidence by the evidence of subsequent writings referring to it and deriving content from that source. There are enough of those writings that scholars have put together a version (or versions) that they think it must be like.

Q is a "sayings gospel," that is, a record of many of Jeshua's sayings or teachings. This is similar to the "Book of Thomas," which helps explain my attraction to Gary Renard. Not only did we know each other, we were trying to achieve many of the same things in our life's work of that incarnation.

In a later session, I asked Ahtun Re who my spirit guide is. After a few quiet moments where he was obviously meditating or searching for that information, he told me that it was the gospel John. That validated what I sensed with Cindy.

I once asked Ahtun Re about a memory I had as a small child. I think I was probably about four, sitting on the floor in the corner of my bedroom by myself. I had a pencil, and was rolling it around by just pointing my finger at it and intending it to roll. At the time it seemed unremarkable. It was just another thing to do when I was bored and alone. I didn't think it strange until I remembered it years later, and thereafter never shared it with anyone. I described it to Ahtun Re and asked if it was true. He took a moment, then asked where this had happened, the specific address. Then after another few silent moments he confirmed it. Part of what prompted me to ask about this specific incident was that in Dr. Kautz's book A New Jesus, he described that the very young Jeshua would amuse himself and friends by animating clay figurines that they had made.

For most of us, the limited ego mind prevents us from experiencing the phenomenon of psychokinetics. In my egoless innocence of that moment, moving the pencil with only intention was possible. Unfortunately, as we learn the ego's lessons, such things become "impossible." Jeshua, on the other hand, eventually achieved a state of no ego, which means no limits. Walking on water, changing water into wine, and even raising the dead is possible when you live from your unlimited mind.

My meetings with remarkable people, and learning of my long distant past, resulted from being willing to "keep doing the next right thing." Grace led me on this journey, introducing me to the right people at the right time in ways I could never have predicted. And, I am grateful for my new friends!

Chapter 8

Using Your Constant Companion: The Observing Mind

PERHAPS you are beginning to have a better appreciation for the split mind we all possess. On one hand is the ego, with all its illusions of control and its games that ultimately lead to suffering. On the other hand is the Mind that you and everyone else shares, reflecting the infinite truth of love and compassion. Now that you are aware of this split mind, you can observe it within yourself and become even more aware of the choices we all have. Let me share with you some experiences, thoughts and observations about the qualities of this split mind.

One of my very early memories dates from when I was about five years old. Being from the Midwest, we had a basement that often became our play area when the weather did not accommodate being outdoors. My sister, five years older, had a friend over who was "playing school" with her. They were using a portable chalkboard as a prop to pretend they were in school. I'm sure I made quite a pest of myself wanting to participate.

Exasperated, my sister handed me a piece of chalk and challenged me to demonstrate to them that I could, indeed, do something that demonstrated my ability to play school. She expected me to fail, so she'd be justified in sending me on my way. I experienced quite a bit of panic when the chalk was handed to me, a five-year-old's version of stage fright. Nevertheless I took the chalk, not quite sure what I would do with it. Somehow I knew how to surrender to the moment, and something changed. I became an observer, and my hand began to move, as if by magic, and produce something on the chalkboard. My sister recognized what I was producing before I did, and exclaimed, "Oh, a hat!" Then I recognized the perfect, simple little baseball hat that I just drawn, but I didn't understand how that happened.

Years later, in the eighth grade I had an art assignment to draw anything that I wanted on an 8 x 10 sheet of white construction paper. I remember sitting at the kitchen table, desperate for an idea when I remembered drawing the hat. So, pencil in hand, I just decided to "allow it" to draw. It drew. At first I didn't recognize the result, but soon it became apparent that I'd sketched a cow's head, straight-on and close-up. I got an A for the assignment, but still wonder where that choice of subject came from.

Later, in my high school basketball playing days, I remember many times when I experienced this observing phenomenon. Particularly when I was playing well, I experienced being in the "zone" where performance becomes automatic and instinctive, not requiring thought or conscious decision. The action seems to slow down and everything seems easier. In my teenage bravado I gladly accepted the praise for high-performance moments, but also felt awkward about being complimented for things I didn't really feel responsible for.

Looking back, I now understand the goodwill of Grace is always available if we can allow it. On each person's unique journey, particular circumstances will arise that allow access to the gift that Grace is constantly offering. Everyone can benefit by learning to train their mind to be available for the gift. It may be hard to swallow at times, but every moment is perfect in providing access to the next lesson that each individual is ready for. Even if you choose the path the ego offers, the benevolent karma of grace immediately "resets" the next moment to give you the opportunity to choose differently. There is always an opportunity to choose the truth of love and honesty instead of the deceit of the ego.

The icon of the "laughing Buddha" I use in my work symbolizes awareness of the split mind. You can watch Grace offer all that you need at any moment, or you can watch the ego offer its hopeless games. As you grow in awareness, you become more amused than tempted by the ego's absurd offerings. Grace offers everything; the ego only offers limits.

Much of meditation is about training your mind to recognize and choose between these opposing perspectives. Much of what we do in clinical hypnosis has the same objective. In fact, there are many paths that can help you develop this perspective, but the method you choose is less important than simply appreciating your desire to become more aware of your own mind's workings.

The "inner observer" is an infinite part of your mind that transcends all time and all limits. It watched your birth and it will watch your death, and it remains at peace regardless of what is going on in your thoughts, feelings, and interactions with the world around you.

An extreme example is that of the Buddhist monk Thich Quan Duc, whose June 1963 self-immolation made the front cover of magazines all over the world. David Halberstam won a Pulitzer for International Reporting in 1964 for coverage of the strife in Vietnam, including his eyewitness report on the event. Today there is a YouTube video showing the monk setting himself ablaze, then quietly sitting there until he falls over dead. Halberstam reported on the eerie serenity displayed by the monk, who was protesting the treatment of Buddhist monks by the South Vietnamese government.

Thich Quan Duc was known to be an enlightened soul, and because he was acting in love and compassion and felt no attachment to worldly things, his fellow Buddhists did not consider it a suicide. After the self-immolation his remains were put through a regular cremation where his heart would not burn. It was displayed in a shrine until it was confiscated by the government and now resides in the Federal Reserve Bank of Viet Nam.

I consider this to be a radical example of what is possible when a clear-thinking mind observes, with correct perspective, the insanity of this dimension. He may not have been laughing but he was at peace. His only turmoil was that so many whom he loved were confused, and their confusion caused their suffering. Grace provides comfort even in such exceptional circumstances.

In my work with DID clients who have an ISH (inner self helper), I came to think of the ISH as that individual's voice of Grace. The voice of the ISH was always kind, never angry. The peace emanating from the client was palpable in the room every time the ISH's presence was known. The responses from the ISH were always truthful, and the ISH's only distress was due to the suffering of the client. It was their internal "laughing Buddha."

This is available to all of us. You can learn to use clear thinking to step away from the insanity of the ego mind that thinks in terms of separation, boundaries and limits. You can make yourself available to the infinite blessings that Grace offers at every moment. If motivated by love and honesty, finding grace is as easy as drawing your next breath.

"All suffering is in the mind and when you learn how to think clearly all suffering ends."

A Course in Miracles is the most efficient mind training tool I know of that can teach you to do this.

In the meantime:

Be grateful.

Keep doing the next right thing based on love and honesty.

And if you make a mistake, simply forgive and resume.

CHAPTER 9

In the Beginning...

CONSIDERING the thoughts and ideas that I've shared so far, the question arises: How did all of this begin? Let me share with you my version of Adam and Eve.

Since the physical universe is a projection of thought by the collective mind, Adam represents the idea of separation from God. Our true nature is created in the image of God: infinite, perfect and complete. The Garden of Eden represents our true nature; the gift of everything has been given to us. In that state, there can be no fear or anxiety.

But Adam represents a "what if" scenario: What if separation was possible? What if I could be separate from my creator? What if I could claim control and responsibility for my happiness? What would that look like? What would the consequences be? With his inherent gift of free will, Adam can take a bite of that speculative apple. Instead of remaining one with All, he becomes one with the idea of pursuing something outside himself.

Yet since separation from our Creator can't really happen, we can only explore the illusions that result from the thought of separation. With the thought of separation we create the thought of a boundary between God and us. We create boundaries. We begin projecting thoughts of untruth, which includes the concept of boundaries that define finite: the ideas of "this and that," "you and me," and "past, present and future." With separation come beginnings and endings, growth and decay, life and death, and creation inextricably paired with destruction. Our thoughts and concepts are now off the mark of infinite truth. We have "sinned" in the sense of falling into illusion, and "the wages of sin is death."

Adam also symbolizes the masculine form or energy that asserts, controls, and tries to dominate. Since the realm of separated thought requires polarity, Eve symbolizes the energy that accepts, receives, and surrenders. This is the yin and yang that permeates everything in this dimension. When the illusion of separation started with Adam, the illusion of return was simultaneously created with the symbol of Eve. In that sense, Eve is a derivative of Adam. It is an illusion of return because separation itself can only be an illusion.

Central to the thoughts that create the finite dimension is the illusion of time. We have time divided into the illusions of past, present and future. But with even a little reflection most people can perceive the illusory nature of both the past and future, and that is why we have developed the spiritual practice of "living in the now." This can be the key to transcendence of illusion, because it leads you to experience life from your mind's perspective instead of your physical senses. Your mind is where your capacity to know the truth directly exists. Like hearing thunder after seeing lightning, your physical senses can offer you partial reflections or symbols of truth, but only through an interpretation process that's fundamentally distorting.

Any stimulation of our senses travels from one place to another. Sound waves travel from a generating event and stimulate our auditory system, sending signals that are interpreted neurologically. Similar activity occurs with the experience of light through our visual system. All our sensory systems thus give us "second-hand news" about our separated condition, seeming to affirm it at every step. But however we may try, it is impossible to reconcile the speed of light with the speed of sound waves to define a "now" in this dimension.

Our confused and guilty ego-mind is trying mightily to re-create what it already has. Having turned away from infinity and love, everything the ego creates reflects its finite nature. Instead of simply accepting the gift of everything, the ego settles for asserting illusory control over its shattered world. Simply said, the ego is insane.

Ages of the Illusion

The Garden of Eden provided all that we need, but the ego seduced us into thinking maybe that is not enough. It seduced us with the idea we could be in control of it as well. So, we go from simply gathering what we need to planting and raising crops. We corral and manage livestock, harvest and store the products. We like to think we are in control of these processes. But everything in the finite dimension ultimately fails or goes away, so we struggle to remain in control as we battle against drought, flood, disease or infestations. All ego-directed plans require struggle against flaws, failures, and limits. Of course, the ego cannot let you recognize the true problem, so we pursue "progress" through more effort, manipulation, and innovations. We apply more of the masculine energy of Adam.

Another of our great historical evolutions was the Industrial Age, in which machinery facilitated the ego's agenda on a more massive and grandiose scale. Of course every step on this path creates more details and data that have to be learned and managed. When minor or major disasters occur, from the breakdown of an automobile to catastrophic global climate change, the ego seduces us into the idea that the solution is to improve our methods, do more, and innovate further. All of this produces massive amounts of data we have to manage and control.

Currently we find ourselves in the age of computers and information. The ego now suggests that our salvation lies in better information management and ever faster digital communications. But these innovations come with their own catastrophic potential, from texting while driving to cyberterrorism.

A Ponzi Scheme

Starting with that initial idea of separation represented by Adam, we convinced ourselves that we were adrift in a chaotic world that constantly requires management via endless decision-making. With the idea of the initial separation arose the appearances of this and that, and the requirement of choosing between them. And from those decisions arise an ever-increasing range of options and choices requiring more judgments and decisions. Each of those decisions continues to grow exponentially upon each other, creating a pyramid of illusions and untruth. I call this the Ponzi scheme of the ego.

Like any Ponzi scheme, this pyramid will ultimately fail. From this perspective, I view human history as the record of this pyramid scheme. Every step into it threatens to expose the truth of its ultimate failure and demise. And that requires the players to become even more sophisticated in disguising the lies they tell themselves about ultimately achieving "success."

One of my favorite passages from ACIM is "you need do nothing." At any moment, any step of the Ponzi scheme of the ego, you can choose the path of Eve. You can surrender instead of control, exchange grandiosity for gratitude, and align with God instead of attempting to manipulate the world. By believing that you "need" to do something, you create and project the illusion that there is something to be done. When you fully accept that all is given, there is no need to do anything. With that understanding, you will naturally express gratefulness for all you've been given.

Before and After...

One of my favorite Buddhist expressions is *"Before enlightenment, chop wood and carry water; after enlightenment, chop wood and carry water.*" This means that while you will always go through the motions of dealing with the illusory world, there is a profound difference in doing them with awareness. While you are in the middle of the pyramid scheme of the ego, your decisions and actions serve the ego. When you become enlightened, your decisions and actions begin to serve the truth. Now you are paradoxically serving the understanding that decisions and judgments ultimately are not necessary. Ultimately, "you need do nothing."

The work begins with being honest about where you are at any given time, responding to worldly circumstances in the most loving way. This means you now have the understanding that you and everyone else have everything you or they inwardly need. In this sense, "there is nothing to fear." Those who are afraid are simply confused, and not a threat to you in any way. You understand that those who are afraid are simply seduced by the absurd idea they need something they don't already have. And you easily forgive their confusion — and your own.

CHAPTER 10

Sex With a Mission

SEXUALITY provides some of the most dramatic experiences in our life for the expression or reflection of either the Truth or the ego. Free will places you in charge of which path you choose. This is an arena wherein it becomes so apparent that confusion leads to suffering, and clear thinking leads to happiness. Nothing causes more fear, shame and guilt for most of us than sex, yet nothing offers more opportunities for joy and personal validation.

Your ultimate truth is that you were created in the image of God, and endowed with all the qualities of infinite perfection and happiness that implies. When you live and reflect your truth in the face of the ego's most diligent objections, joy can be the only outcome. When you stand fully revealed, fully exposed with only honest and loving intentions, you are reflecting truth more powerfully than in any other ordinary experience of life. When individuals are able to share intimacy of this kind, it becomes a synergetic experience that transcends any joy known alone.

Ultimately we are one with all others. When we honestly reflect that truth via the coital experience of connection, we are revealing who we really are. It is no coincidence that our greatest symbol of creativity in this dimension, the birth of a child, is a product of this profound intimacy.

On the other hand, the ego is ingenious in its relentless seductions. It takes every opportunity to steer you into shame or guilt. "How could you like that? How could you do that? Don't you dare reveal these things to anyone, including yourself," says the ego.

Is there any greater temptation to be dishonest when, in the heat of biological passion, we lie to ourselves about our readiness to have a child? Procreation via the ego either validates one's power motive or becomes an excuse for shame and guilt. Or perhaps we use our sexuality to exert power and control over our partners, instead of love and sharing. Attraction and seduction, experienced as a form of power, may be pursued as an ego-driven path to an illusion of happiness.

Let's also consider the effects of the Ponzi scheme of the ego as it pertains to our sexuality. At the beginning there is the masculine and the feminine, fundamental elements of duality that clearly differentiate "this" from "that." But even that duality can be subdivided into more variations. It is very easy for the ego to judge or condemn any of these variations, instead of loving and accepting them all as gifts of life. Being able to reveal your own variations with a trusted partner, without fear or any other of the ego's power games is a fairly rare experience.

It is well understood in psychology that each individual psyche has both masculine and feminine aspects. In dream analysis it is understood that most dreams that include characters of the opposite sex are representing the dreamer's own mind. When a man dreams of a woman, he is generally projecting his own feminine aspects onto her. The opposite is true when a woman dreams of a man. But no one is exclusively male or female; we are all unique combinations of these energies, and there are many variations on our basic theme. The ego would have you judge or condemn some of these variations, or conversely, use them to fuel a grandiose illusion of yourself.

Your true self can only celebrate the life given to you, regardless of your sexual variations. The path of love and acceptance of yourself and others leads to the experience of inner grandeur, not external grandiosity.

Evidence of reincarnation offers some insights here. In his research, Dr. Walter Semkiw has pointed out that a gay person was often the opposite gender in their previous life. In his book, *Born Again: Reincarnation Cases Involving Evidence of Past Lives with Xenoglossy Cases Researched by Ian Stevenson*, he cites the case of a male Japanese Soldier during the occupation of Burma in World War II. This soldier, who was a cook, befriended a Burmese woman who had culinary interests. After this Japanese cook was killed in an Allied strafing run, the cook reincarnated and was born to the Burmese woman he befriended, which demonstrates the principle of reincarnation that we plan lifetimes to be with people we have affection for. Though the cook reincarnated as a woman, she retained the mindset of a man, including an attraction to women, which led this person to become a lesbian.

In Ian Stevenson's research involving 1200 objectively validated reincarnation cases, gender change only occurred in 10 percent of cases, inferring that one's soul has a preferred gender to incarnate in. When one incarnates into a gender that one is not accustomed to, homosexuality, transsexualism and other gender identity issues may occur. As such, any of us may incarnate into a gender we are not used to, which may lead to gender identity issues and homosexuality. We should not judge these conditions, or we may need to experience a lifetime as a homosexual or transsexual based on karma.   Walter has created a website, www.ReincarnationResearch.com, where these and other categories of reincarnation cases can be reviewed.

As noted, in cases where karma is involved, reincarnation affords us the opportunity to transcend that which we may have judged, and to atone by achieving acceptance, compassion and forgiveness.

Dr. Semkiw specifically uses the case of Bruce/Caitlin Jenner. He has postulated that Jenner was female Olympian "Babe" Didrickson in a previous life. Though we do not know whether Jenner's transsexualism was karmic or simply that Jenner was used to female lifetimes, Jenner clearly has suffered a great deal of angst and anxiety over the predicament of this life experience and, at least to some observers, become more honest, truthful, and accepting of her thoughts, feelings, wants and needs. Not only has she experienced these for herself, but she has offered many people the opportunity to transcend the ego with love and acceptance instead of harsh judgment.

Our sexuality is the most intimate personal opportunity to transcend the ego's harsh judgment. When you look in a mirror, love that. When you look at others, love that.

The ego will be relentless in trying to hijack that love to turn it into some illusion of power and control. Understand that the allure, attraction, appeal or desire we feel for others is a reflection of our truth to be connected to all there is. Our ego has us judging and imposing conditions of that desire, which creates the limits with which we defined our desire. It is the ego that says, "I only like this" or "I only like that."

As a collective we have developed conventions about "this" or "that," what is desirable or not. Madison Avenue is highly skilled at using this profound desire we all have and redirecting it towards their desire for their illusions of power and control. In that arena, the grading scale is money, corporate profits. I find it ironic that our sexuality, something that is so individual and personal, is also used on a massive scale as a currency of marketing and in the process also defining what is "good" or "bad," what is "attractive" or what is "unattractive."

It's also easy to see elements of sadomasochism in our sexuality. Remember, sadomasochism simply comes down to the ego's illusory satisfaction that power and control outweigh the suffering created. The greater the suffering, the greater the illusion of power and control and thus the satisfaction it offers. It hurts so good!

In S&M play, people dance with these dynamics. On one hand, our secret desires are revealed to oneself and each other, transcending ordinary and familiar boundaries. The more daring, the more stimulating. Greater risk offers the payoff of more illusory power and control.

Here I would also like to point out different perspectives on the idea of celibacy. There is the ego-version, and there is a version that reflects transcendence of the ego.

Some spiritual practices encourage giving up your sexuality as a sacrifice necessary to gain spiritual development. As a God of love, our infinite source is antithetical to limits. Having to give up anything to achieve everything does not make sense! It is clearly a confusion and seduction of the ego. I do find it reasonable that when people pursue celibacy from that perspective, it often does not go well. Nothing manifest of the ego will ever ultimately work. That is its nature.

On the other hand, someone with good awareness and perspective can reasonably make the choice of celibacy. Remember, we are living in the dimension of illusions, projections or thoughts. As we move up Maslow's hierarchy of needs, we learn to transcend the fear and anxiety the ego offers at every level. When we have transcended fear and anxiety about sexuality, it becomes more of a conscious choice not so influenced by the ego. I have no difficulty accepting that one could choose not to be distracted by sexuality and all the time, energy and effort that it calls for. There is no right or wrong about it. There is only each individual making the choice in the most honest and loving way for them.

On the other end of the spectrum, some have experimented and explored their sexuality outside the conventional rules of monogamous pairing and mating. Here again, there is no absolute right or wrong. The same standard applies: that the individual be as honest, and loving and kind to self and others as they can be. It can be very easy for the ego to seduce us with desire to the point that we delude ourselves about how conscious we actually are. I cannot stress enough how powerful the physical experience of sex with another can be. This power is so readily hijacked by the ego that you have to challenge yourself on the issue of trustworthiness. If you are not intending sexual exclusivity, can you trust another person's ability to cooperate with that choice? Is it worth the risk, considering how powerfully hurt one can be from unconscious sexual behavior?

I think it is clear that society's conventions about rules and taboos regarding sex exist partly to make decisions more conscious and deliberate, when the ego would prefer blind obedience to its seductions. Of course, the ego, being the opportunistic intelligence that it is, can also hijack rules and conventions to foster its own purposes.

Another area of sexual concern is its initiation. Our awareness of our genitals, and the pleasure experienced by stimulating them, is appreciated by most people very early in life. It is often a thoughtless or automatic experience born of our innocence and youth. This evolves to explorations where our curiosity leads to "playing doctor" and other games of sexual curiosity.

Unfortunately, these explorations are often responded to by our parents or caregivers with shaming or even punishment. That gives the ego great neurotic energy to fuel its own games. Clearly, the more children are allowed to get to know themselves this way without fear, shame and guilt, the better. On the other hand, appropriate boundaries are necessary as well to function within society in a healthy way.

As people grow into puberty and early adult life, the drive to procreate and connect intimately also grows. Here again, this evolution should be approached with kindness and honesty. To approach it with fear, intimidation, dishonesty and condemnation only fuels the ego and its neurotic ways. The great gift of our sexuality becomes a powerful source of neurosis in the hands of the ego.

The same basic principles apply here. Be grateful. Your sexuality is one of the most profound ways you get to experience life in this dimension. It is one of the most significant ways you get to experience your "am-ness" and, at the same time, a rich opportunity to experience another and transcend the habit of our separation.

You should proceed in your sexual life by doing the next right thing motivated by love and honesty. Beware that seducing you to believe you can be in control of your happiness is how the ego deceives you. The biology of sexual stimulation can make us feel very good even in dishonest circumstances. But I assure you that the greatest overall sexual satisfaction you can experience will come with love and honesty.

But we are humans with egos. Mistakes will be made. All mistakes are to be approached with compassion and forgiveness. This applies to yourself and all others. There will be many opportunities for the ego to steer you into areas of fear, shame and guilt, but you can learn to lightly brush them aside and chuckle at the ego's antics.

CHAPTER 11

What is Marriage Really About?

CONSIDERING that "all suffering is in the mind and when you learn how to think clearly, all suffering ends," marriage offers some very special lessons about suffering and transcendence.

Sometimes I refer to marriage as a laboratory where we get to use defined ingredients (the partners) and mix them together in order to learn more about indefinable reactions. You can also learn and define different catalysts in regard to their reactions in this laboratory. It can be the crucible that helps us isolate and define the alchemy of the individual and relationships.

A basic paradigm of this book is that life, by its very nature, is an irreconcilable phenomenon. This basic irreconcilability is traced back to the fundamental illusion of separation. The simplest reduction of that illusion is duality: this and that, you and me. At every level, the individual will have conflict with the collective, whether the collective is one other person, or the family, neighborhood, community, state, country or world. Wherever the individual encounters an entity other than himself there will be conflict. Enlightenment, or realizing that you are at one with everything, is attained by transcending all illusions of conflict and separation.

But even at its simplest and most reduced form, conflict is unavoidable. What one thinks, feels, needs and wants will never match exactly what another thinks, feels, needs and wants. Also, even at this most reduced experience of two, all the reflections of the ego as well as all the reflections of Grace and Truth can be seen.

In the marriage laboratory, each individual has the challenge of risking and revealing their true selves. It takes great courage to reveal not just to another but also to yourself what you really think, feel, want and need. This requires the skills of assertiveness.

On the other hand, it is also your job to promote the safety and security that allows your partner to be self-revealing. Thus, listening and empathy are required skills. Assertiveness, listening, and empathy are the basic building blocks of intimacy.

I ask people considering marriage to ponder two questions. One: is there a spark? There doesn't have to be the exaggerated romantic energy that we see in movies and television. But there does have to be this "thing" or attraction, whether it makes sense or not, that says I like this person or I enjoy this person. Two: would you go into business with this person? It's important to realize that intimate partnership requires some of the same dynamics of a partnership in business. Can and will this other person show up to do what they are expected to do? Can you trust them with all of your assets and resources? These may not be the romantic things we like to think about with marriage, but they are absolutely necessary in order for a partnership to work. For this kind of trust, it takes both parties to make it work, but only one party to make it not work.

Let me also point out that as we evolve up Maslow's hierarchy of needs, those needs evolve as well. When we operate at lower levels of the hierarchy, needs are generally more about the more concrete requirements of life. Once we evolve past these, then it's more important that we are able to respond to each other's emotional and spiritual needs. This requires that we define for ourselves what these needs are, not simply mimicking what others have done, such as our parents.

Sometimes I like to explain that the inner adult in both parties has to know how to work together in a reasonable and functional way in order to tend to the business of managing a relationship. On the other hand, the reason we want to be together is because the inner child in both parties likes each other and knows how to have fun together. The "how" of togetherness depends on the capacity of inner adults to manage the business of being together that's founded on the joy of being together.

Once these practical fundamentals are established, emotional and spiritual growth happens with the same basic mechanics of revealing, asserting, and responding in a safe environment. Then we can begin to transcend our separateness and approach an experience of oneness. Now these basic mechanics become even more powerful symbols and reflections. When these skills of assertiveness and responsiveness are pursued with honesty and loving intention, Grace is invited into the experience and miraculous things can happen.

Another basic paradigm of this book is that there are no coincidences. Everything that shows up in your life is exactly the lesson or opportunity at that moment for your spiritual development. The people you encounter, including the special people we develop partnerships with, are not there by accident. The research into reincarnation, as well as my own study, suggests that the people we develop partnerships with are usually people we have been involved with in previous lifetimes. When the student is ready the teacher will appear. Each partner should consider the other partner both their teacher and student. We can be grateful for the lessons provided about honesty, love, compassion and forgiveness.

Remember, there are no victims. When we experience ourselves as victims we are buying into the ego's seduction of the drama triangle. Instead of responding to difficult circumstances as a victim, the more effective response is to ask yourself, "What am I to learn here? What is the lesson about truth, compassion, love and forgiveness that I'm being taught here?" The two of you will continue to grow together in your ability to be honest, compassionate, loving and forgiving.

If you find yourself with a partner who is not willing or able to engage lessons at the same level, your challenge may be to love yourself enough to remove yourself from harm's way, all things considered. It is these lessons that I consider

the most sacred aspect of marriage, leading to your understanding of your true and divine nature. Remember, if anyone is ever unkind they are confused, and you are called to
"forgive them for they know not what they do."

What I have explained above is an oversimplification.
With the ego's help, we make this an extremely complicated
thing. These are the ingredients of high drama that almost
everybody has experienced. Most people are engaged in this
high drama with little conscious awareness. If you are reading this book you are making your unconscious conscious.
You are seeking; many are not. You may be tempted to rescue those who are not seeking. And while it is always your
job to witness truth whenever you can, with loving intention; that is not the same as rescuing. If someone is unwilling
to listen, if they are not seeking, you can trust the dynamics
of God, karma, or Truth to lead them on their path to enlightenment. As they say in AA, "let go and let God." Or as
they say in Al-anon, "detach with love."

Many people are pursuing experiences of connection
and intimacy without understanding why. Our pursuit of
intimacy with another is a reflection of our longing to be one
with everything, one with God. The ego easily hijacks that
for its own purposes. While the institution of marriage has
legitimate purposes, the ego easily seduces us into misusing
those purposes to foster fear, shame and guilt. It's one thing
to have an individual condemn you it's another to have the
community condemn you.

To be blunt, when men and women have sex, children

can happen. Many of our societal rules about sex and marriage were born of that simple fact. Survival of the species required that child-rearing be managed. Particularly when we are operating at the lower levels of Maslow's hierarchy so much of these drivers in our life were of a more unconscious phenomenon. Things are evolving.

One of the most significant things that happened in our evolution is the development of effective birth control. Now we can have sex without the inevitability of procreation; sex can now be specifically and singularly for the pleasure and joy of it. It can be an exquisite celebration of life.

Another aspect of this sexual revolution is that we are creating babies in new and unconventional ways. Now we can utilize surrogates, or even test tubes in the laboratory. And there will be most certainly more developments that create even more possibilities. This requires a greater consciousness and awareness of what we do and why we do it. And the ego is there to create chaos at every step of the way.

The realm of intimate relationship is also affected by increasing longevity. About a century ago, in our society, the average lifespan was around fifty years of age. For the most part, people were not living much beyond the age of normal reproduction. Now most people live well beyond that. The Baby Boomers are done raising their children; now what? I've seen many people struggle with their desire and pursuit of relationship and intimacy using a set of rules that don't really apply to this brave new world.

People may also choose not to partner at all. Some may

feel that their spiritual mission in life is to love everybody without an exclusive intimacy. They are willing to forgo the distractions or confusions one must deal with when we venture into partnership. The ego has an easy time seducing us into believing that we need a "special" person to have a unique experience of special love. The real mission with our partners is to experience and practice love in a way that develops our skills at loving in general.

The whole concept of "special" is an easy tool for the ego to create distinction and separation. Conflict is one of the ego's major means to enforce separateness and the "special" people in our world provides the ego with "special" opportunities for conflict.. The basic instruction to "love your enemies" is about transcending conflict with love, thus transcending the illusion of separation. On the other hand, there are those who do not have partners but wish that they did. It is impossible to list all the ways and all the lessons that are being taught in various circumstances, but we can trust there are no accidents. The individual's job, whether in a special relationship or not, is always to be honest, have loving intentions and keep doing the next right thing. By doing this, we allow our infinite Source to lead us where it would have us go, and have us be with whom it would have us be.

CHAPTER 12

What is Parenting Really About?

THE FAMILY that a child is born into is not a biological accident. Every child is born into a circumstance that serves their karmic evolution and purpose, setting up the lessons their life will afford them. Each child provides opportunities for the parents in their development as well — providing another perspective on the idea that "when the student is ready the teacher will appear." In fact, family provides the most profound demonstration of this truth.

The child enters this dimension with an awareness, albeit mostly unconscious, that their true nature is of an infinite quality. The world they are entering is finite; thus begins the interplay of those irreconcilable conditions. The parents, being adults who have more or less adapted to this finite dimension, are tasked with the mission to teach the child how to manage life with limits.

There is still a part of us all that wants and feels without limits. This is a reflection of the deep knowledge within of our infinite nature. In my profession we sometimes refer to that part of us that wants and feels without limits as the "inner child." Becoming an adult means, in part, learning to practically manage the limits of this dimension.

So the job of parenting involves teaching the child how to do that. The most we can hope for is the ability to stay connected to the "inner child" who knows what we deeply feel and want, while our adult consciousness provides problem-solving strategies that are responsive to those feelings and desires. When the Buddhists say, "life is suffering," they are acknowledging that our infinite nature cannot really be reconciled with this finite realm, and the inevitable result is suffering. The laughing Buddha understands the absurdity of this endeavor even while he participates in it.

How It Begins

A child enters this dimension completely dependent, unable to survive without a parent or caretaker. This condition reflects our profound need to stay connected, despite the illusion of separateness, and is thus just as essential to who and what we are as our individual ego-identity. I find it interesting that we experience this total dependency when we are at our most innocent. Another way to put it is that when the ego has the least influence on us, we experience our need for connection most intensely.

Like individuals, families experience Maslow's hierarchy of needs. When the family is primarily concerned about concrete survival issues, they have a very different dynamic than a family that has ascended to concerns about their emotional and spiritual well-being.

Most middle-class adults in our culture have ascended

that far. Unlike their parents or grandparents, they grew up in a world where the concerns about having food on the table, clothes on their back, and a roof over their head were not paramount. While blessed not to have those primal anxieties, they've faced more intangible challenges of personal growth and spiritual fulfillment that their parents were not familiar with, and consequently couldn't teach well. Parenting challenges can thus change with the passage of time and societal evolution.

A family is a "system" on a continuum where one end of the continuum reflects the focus of the desires and well-being of the individual, and the other end of the continuum reflects the desires and well-being of the whole. The polarities of the continuum reflect the inherent irreconcilable nature of a separated dimension. Prioritizing the individual's needs and concerns results in a very different system dynamics than a system that prioritizes the needs and desires of the collective.

When families were more concerned about achieving concrete survival, traditional paternalism reigned. When the father was the ultimate arbiter and authority figure, parenting mostly taught children to fit within an authoritative system. Do as you're told; don't talk back; children are to be seen and not heard are familiar ideas of that system. How the children felt, and what their individual mission on earth might prove to be, was not a primary concern.

As we evolve beyond concrete needs, concerns for a child's feelings, well-being, and inner development become more prominent. A child, being dependent and vulnerable, is easily defined as a victim. And it's very easy for parents to be defined as either heroic rescuers or despicable perpetrators. As children get older and become more responsible for their own choices, they begin to participate independently in the ego's seductions, including the drama triangle and the internalization of shame and guilt.

I consider empathy to be the most important parenting skill. Considering all the dynamics that I've been explaining so far, I hope it is clear that there can be no strict rules about parenting. It always requires adapting the lessons the parent is trying to teach to the unique and specific circumstances of the child, with love and honesty.

In infancy, the child is completely dependent and has no capacity to make decisions. As children grow, their ability to make choices increases. So parents gradually dole out decision-making to their children. This process takes constant vigilance and adjustment. It is impossible to do this perfectly, and everyone involved will have many opportunities to practice forgiveness —a fundamental skill of being a happy and functional adult.

The transition from child to adult is one of dependence to independence, and the ego has many opportunities to insert its insanity in this perilous process on both sides of the parent-child equation. Sometimes there are profound difficulties, even abuse. Karma has provided the conditions in which to learn the forgiveness lessons that heal any wounds. And the benefits of those lessons may extend beyond the family.

Often parents will report an experience of profound love when they see their baby for the first time. This is an example of the love we have for each other when the ego has minimal interference. It is sometimes a great challenge when the child becomes older, and consequently has a more developed ego, to remember that original love and devotion. The parents' own ego issues interfere as well. And there may be times when certain difficult circumstances require separating from one another. Perhaps a parent consumed with ego dysfunction is abusive, or a child becomes unmanageable, requiring resources beyond what the family can offer. The variations of the drama are too numerous to list here.

But the lesson of every family situation, whatever confusion, unkindness, or abuse is at hand, is that all is to be forgiven. Every step of the process challenges us to practice empathy. It is only by understanding each other as fully as possible that we find the healthiest responses. In all cases, be grateful. Even amidst the worst turmoil, you are being given the opportunity to evolve along your spiritual path.

Parenting is one of the most sacred endeavors a person can take on. Not everyone will be called to do it. But if you are, you will be teaching others to reconcile the contradictory aspects of their finite and infinite natures — how to be healthy individuals within the collective of the family, society, and world at large. This means that everyone involved will be learning gratitude, honesty, and forgiveness.

CHAPTER 13

It's Curtains For The Ego!

"ALL THE WORLD'S A STAGE," said Shakespeare, "and all the men and women merely players; they have their exits and their entrances..." I wonder if he was contemplating reincarnation when he wrote that.

In my younger days as a social worker and psychotherapist, I thought I was just learning how to perform in whatever professional circumstance came to me. In looking back, it is clear to me that there were no coincidences. There were several false starts in different professions before I found myself in social work school. There were several options in social work besides psychotherapy along the way. I found myself pursuing information and ideas not typical for many psychotherapists. And then I found clients synchronistically showing up in my practice.

A more recent chain of events involves my new friend Suzanne Peyton. I have been doing a few workshops over the past few years introducing my colleagues to the phenomenon of reincarnation, and its implications to our work as psychotherapists. My local newspaper has a weekly column that introduces authors in our area. Suzanne has written a book revealing her discovery that she is the reincarnation of her great-grandmother, with a great deal of documented evidence to support that assertion. Her story is so compelling that Hollywood is interested in making a movie of her story.

Our meeting is just another suggestion to me that there are patterns or mechanisms at work that validate there are no accidents or coincidences. But who writes the script and why?

In a word, curiosity. Here's what I mean by that. We were created in the image of God, with all the infinite perfection of love that implies. Perfect love implies free will. You cannot compel or force love; force and love are incompatible mechanisms. Also, God is of an infinite nature and that means we are of an infinite nature. Infinity, by its very definition, transcends everything, including any concept of finite. We don't really choose one or the other, as the ego would like you to believe.

To put it simply, only infinite things ultimately matter. All finite things end, and are comparatively insignificant. Here we are, living an earthly life under the pretense that we could be separate from God and each other. Free will, a product of love, allows us to have these ideas. So we write our scripts exploring separation, very much like playwrights write their scripts following their curiosities. Each unique character is an amalgam of our idea of separation (the ego) and the truth of our infinite, perfect essence.

Recognize that all the other people you encounter are necessary for you to explore and fulfill your curiosity about some aspect of life. At any moment, you can't be you without every other person being who they are at that moment. In a separated world, there can't be a protagonist without an antagonist. And neither of them can be who they are without the foils, settings and subplots necessary to fully explore their personal drama.

When this is fully understood, we can appreciate even our enemies. And then, loving and even forgiving our enemies will seem less difficult. We can even be grateful for them.

The depth psychologist Carl Jung once said, "I would rather be whole than good." He understood that we cannot fully know ourselves unless we embrace our dualism. To be "good" in this existence requires also being "bad." as well. It is only through our recognition of that split that we eventually come to the realization that we really do not want the dualistic choice. Eventually we will choose differently.

When you fully understand these choices, forgiveness is understood to be a dismissal of the dualistic mind altogether, not an acceptance or tolerance of the "bad" side of the dualistic equation. Forgiveness that is not a release of the dualistic mind actually strengthens the ego's seduction. The ego can misuse forgiveness as just another tool to help us press ahead with the insane idea of making this irreconcilable dimension workable.

That is, the ego would have you believe there are options within the dualistic mind that can work. We will experiment with all the ego's seductions until we fully appreciate the fallacy of its seductions, and recognize its absurdity. Then real forgiveness is understood as appreciating that people pursue their happiness the best way they know how. Any unkindness results from the deal they think they have to make to achieve their happiness. This is a typical confusion resulting from trying to make dualism work.

Our egocentric expressions are to be simply forgiven because they are of a finite nature and ultimately don't really matter. Expressions of our true nature are only to be celebrated. Some people's drama with life are so charged by ego that they are hard to forgive. Forgiving Hitler for the way he pursued and expressed his pursuit of happiness is quite a challenge, but there will always be another dangerous demagogue on the horizon to provide us with a similar opportunity.

A Forgiving Technique

Let me offer this technique I use for forgiveness. Perhaps you have a favorite actor that you know to be a genuinely kind and good person offstage or offscreen. And this actor may have played a character that was truly despicable. In an interview, that actor may have acknowledged how interesting, curious, or entertaining it was to play such a character.

Start looking at everyone that way, including yourself. At the extreme of villainy, there are people willing to do sadistic things in the name of making this dualistic dimension work for them. They may gladly sacrifice you and others for their apparent gain. They have lost touch with the awareness that everyone here dies, and ultimately there is no satisfaction in a finite world. If anyone thinks this way, then they are simply confused.

Even the most destructive confusion is rooted in the pursuit of a happy life. How much abuse can or should be tolerated is a practical question; sometimes we have to remove ourselves from harm. Sometimes we have to confront another's unkind confusion. Sometimes we even have to lock them up!

But instead of simply condemning those who do harm, we can approach them with empathy and compassion. I truly believe that when you regard someone's confusion with empathy and compassion instead of fear and condemnation, you are working with your own karma to reduce the number of lessons you will have to learn. With empathy and compassion, you can learn your lessons through the experiences of another.

Karma is not a punishment. In fact, it is another expression of love that Truth offers you, allowing your recognition of how you are using free will. Whatever thoughts the ego may seduce you with, whatever curiosities you may have about experiencing dualism, karma will compliment you with instructive circumstances. You will be given all the opportunities you need to "choose once again." You will be given every opportunity you need to learn you are a child of God.

So, as the Buddhists say, "All suffering is in the mind and when you learn how to think clearly all suffering ends." We can consciously engage in this mind training, or we can let karma lead us to the readiness to make that conscious choice. The only thing we have to lose is the suffering!

For me, and many others, Gary Renard's *The Disappearance of the Universe* was invaluable to help me take advantage of the mind training offered by *A Course in Miracles*.

Let these tools help you draw the curtains to a close on the stage where the ego performs. Let these tools lead you past all your curiosities about dualism in the most efficient way. Learn to be a "passer-by" sitting in the audience watching the absurd drama of fear and limitations, resting in the fact that the infinite cannot be undone by some tiny, mad idea of finite.

In the meantime, what ever your path may be:

Be grateful!

Keep doing the next right thing with love and honesty!

If you make a mistake, simply forgive and resume!

Acknowledgments

Sometimes I joke that God has a sense of humor, and one of the ways I know this is because I was inspired to write this book — even though I don't like to write and I am not very good at it. So the only way this could work is with the help and support of many key people.

First of all, I would like to thank my editor, D. Patrick Miller. He graciously shared my foxhole on the frontlines of this endeavor. Not only was his expertise in writing needed, but I also discovered that the writer/editor relationship is a very interesting, unique and dynamic experience. His professionalism and guidance made this possible. And, by the way, he was also the editor of one of the most revered books on my shelf, *The Disappearance of the Universe*. Additionally, he has a thorough knowledge of *A Course In Miracles* as well as knowledge and experience with psychology including Dissociative Identity Disorders, one of my areas of expertise. Funny how that works!

As you will learn in this book, Gary Renard, author of *The Disappearance of the Universe*, and his wife Cindy have had a profound effect on my life. Not only did his book change my life, but also their kindness, encouragement and support cannot be overstated in the production of this book. Your friendship means so much to me and I thank you both!

Through Cindy Lora-Renard's encouragement I got to work with Kevin Ryerson and his "support staff from the other side," so to speak. This book would not have happened with out my experiences with Kevin, and I am grateful.

I also want to thank Dr. Walter Semkiw for his courageous research and sharing of his personal story. Dr. Semkiw's meticulous and professional methodology brings a discipline to the research on reincarnation that cannot be dismissed. I am personally grateful that he reviewed and supported this book with suggestions and amendments where I am referencing his work.

Dr. Stephen Karpman, creator of the "Drama Triangle," has generously given me permission to refer to his work. Not only is the Drama Triangle a tool I use throughout this book, but it has also been useful throughout my career. I not only thank him personally, but I want to thank him for his contribution to our profession.

Most importantly, I am grateful for the love and support of my wife, Karen. At first glance it may seem unusual, and maybe it is, that she does not share my passion for psychology and spirituality. Yet she has never flinched in her support of me following these passions. In some ways that makes her support even more remarkable. On the other hand, I have come to learn we have partnered before in previous lifetimes, so it makes sense that she is so good at it! Nevertheless, in this lifetime, I am grateful for all of your support and can't imagine anyone but you being my partner. I love you and I thank you!

Made in the USA
Lexington, KY
08 November 2017